THE MONK WHO SHOOK THE WORLD

STORIES OF FAITH AND FAME
Edited by Cecil Northcott

Friends or Enemies?

THE MONK
WHO SHOOK THE WORLD

The Story of Martin Luther

by
CYRIL DAVEY

LUTTERWORTH PRESS
LONDON

First published 1960
Second impression 1961
Third impression 1963
Fourth impression 1966
Fifth impression 1970

COPYRIGHT © 1960 CYRIL DAVEY

ISBN 0 7188 0869 x

PRINTED IN GREAT BRITAIN
PHOTOLITHO BY EBENEZER BAYLIS AND SON, LTD.
THE TRINITY PRESS, WORCESTER, AND LONDON

CONTENTS

1

THE BOY WHO SAW THE DEVIL

AWAY behind him, across the fields, when he turned round the boy could see the towers and spires rising behind the city walls of Mansfeld. Somewhere amongst the crowded houses his mother and father would be looking for him at this moment, wandering through the narrow streets where the wooden houses almost touched each other as they leaned forward over the roadway. His father, Hans Luther, would be grumbling at having to leave the foundry, certain that his workmen would put down their tools the moment he was out of sight. His mother would be muttering prayers to St. Anne, their family saint, as she asked the neighbours if they had seen young Martin since the morning.

Little Martin trudged on, hungry and tired, almost wishing that he had not run away after all. The forest was only a few hundred yards ahead and he very nearly turned back to the town. A movement in the undergrowth made him jump with fear. It might be a squirrel—or it might be a nasty-tempered elf. He saw nothing when he looked and, squaring his shoulders, he marched towards the trees, a solid, stumpy little boy in rough, homespun clothes. A few minutes later the woods closed round about him, and he felt suddenly cold and frightened. His mother had often talked about seeing gnomes, elves and goblins in the forest when she had been collecting wood for the fire. Everybody in Martin's time believed firmly in the mischievous "little people" who stole eggs, turned milk sour and put spells on people they did not like, just as they believed in witches and wizards who caused sickness, made thunderstorms and sent plagues into the towns and villages of Germany.

Though he had run away from home, feeling sulky and bad-tempered because his father had beaten him for not doing as well as he should have done at school, it took the little boy a long time to gather his courage together and trudge through the trees. But, to the end of his life, Martin would always have plenty of courage, and no one would be able to say he did not face danger with a stout heart, even when he knew well enough that many people were only too ready to see him killed. Those days, however, were still a long way off. Martin was, as yet, only a little boy who had run away and was already beginning to wish he had not done anything so silly. His legs ached. The darkness began to steal across the sky. Thorns whipped his face and hands. Looking round desperately, he found he had lost the path. He stumbled on, frightened and weary, until at last he fell over, tripping on a trailing root, and lay still, too tired to get up.

"Please help me, St. Anne!" he cried. "If you save me from the evil spirits I will light a candle in front of your altar when I get home. You've helped my father to grow wealthy, and looked after us all this time . . . protect me now in this awful forest. . . ." He was still talking to his family saint when he fell asleep. He had no doubt, next morning, when a friendly woodman found him and took him home, that the mother of the Virgin Mary, to whom he had spoken, had heard his prayer and kept him safe. But he never ran away again. In the long, dangerous days ahead he preferred to stand his ground, facing trouble when it came.

*   *   *

Martin Luther was born almost five hundred years ago and grew up in central Germany. In those days Germany was not one single country but a collection of small States each ruled by dukes or princes, all of whom tried to make sure that their own State was more powerful or more important than the rest. Hans Luther, Martin's father, had moved from the village farm where he grew up to the mines and, before Martin was born, he had made enough money out of mining, digging the coal out of the deep pits with his own hands, working with roughly-made picks, hammers and shovels, to become the owner of half a dozen small foundries. By the time he was fifteen Martin had lived in four widely separated towns, going to school at Mansfeld, Magdeburg and Eisenach.

Schools, of course, were run by the Church. Teachers were monks or priests and, in some schools, there was as much time spent at church services as there was in lessons. In those days all of Western Europe worshipped in the Roman Catholic way. The Pope was the Head of the Church. Rome was the greatest city in the world. Bishops and archbishops were at least as important as dukes and princes. The Protestant Churches did not exist, for no one dared to protest even at the things which ordinary people felt were wrong with the Church to which they belonged.

Martin loved school, both the lessons he learned and the church services to which he had to go. There was not much history or geography in German schools of those days. German itself was not taught at all, and mathematics took little time. The real subject was Latin and every schoolboy learnt to speak it fluently and well. It was very important that they should. A German travelling to Italy or England would find hardly anyone who could speak his own tongue, but Latin was spoken everywhere. Lawyers used it in the court-rooms. Governments and kings wrote to each other, and scholars wrote their books in it. Above all, it was the language of the Church, for all services were conducted in Latin and the Bible itself had never been translated into German—or into English, either.

Midday was the worst moment in school for Martin. As the bell rang, books were put away and the monk who taught them looked round the class. The boy who had made most mistakes in his Latin shuffled awkwardly, but it was no use trying to get out of it. As the monk called him out the class began to laugh. The teacher took a donkey's mask and tied it on to the boy's head. It was worse than a dunce's cap, for he had to wear it as he moved round the school until the next day came, when it was presented to someone worse than himself. There was only one other way of getting rid of it. No one might speak anything but Latin in school. If the *asinus*, the boy with the donkey's head, could discover someone whispering to his neighbour in German he could take him to the teacher and get rid of his monstrous head at once, for it would be put straight away over the head of the ignorant lad who preferred to speak his own language—until he too could get rid of it.

This was not the only way mistakes were punished. There were beatings, too—but they were always saved up to the end of the week. Martin never forgot the time when he was given fifteen strokes of the birch on one single day, as a result of a week of careless work. In spite of all this, he loved school and was one of the best Latin scholars in his class. His father, who had beaten him so hard that he ran away, grew more proud of him as the years went by, and talked to his wife about the great man young Martin would one day become.

"That's what comes of having brains," said Hans, thinking of the way he had made his own way in the world as well as young Martin's reports from the monks.

Margarita Luther smiled gently. "Maybe so, Hans," she answered. "*I* think it's because St. Anne cares for us so well." St. Anne was the patron saint of all miners, and none of the family ever forgot to pray to her each day.

*   *   *

There were times when Martin was worried about the endless prayers he had to say. His mother and father, and the monks and priests who taught him, always spoke of God as if He were a long way off, angry and impatient with men and women. They sometimes called Him "The Thunderer", and Martin was often too frightened to pray to Him at all. That was why he usually prayed to Jesus, or, if he wanted something very badly, to Mary the Mother of Jesus or to St. Anne. Usually, however, Martin found the Church was full of interest. He loved its services, attending Mass each day, and liked best of all the times when he was allowed to share in the colourful processions which marched through the town on saints' days and holy days, led by the bishop or the priests in their brilliant robes.

On his way home from school, like all the other boys, he would stop from time to time to watch a monk—a newcomer to one of the monasteries—carrying a sack through the streets, begging bread for his fellow-monks. The boys smiled knowingly at each other when they saw townspeople and shop-keepers angrily refuse to give him any help, knowing that their parents muttered angrily about the way the churches and monasteries were always begging for money or food. At other times, Martin waited near the door of the convent and looked at the group of sick people lying outside. Some were old, others pitted with smallpox and many shook with old age or muttered to themselves as if they were mad. All of them had been brought by relatives or friends, to sit or stand there until the bell of the convent rang for the services of Vespers. That was the moment for healing, so people believed. Now and again, when the bell tolled, someone would shamble off as though he really had been partly cured and Martin would go home in great excitement to tell his mother and father what he had seen. On one special occasion, when he was quite small and the convent was shadowed with the falling darkness, Martin was quite certain that he saw a devil fly out of the mouth of one of the sufferers. He was so frightened

that he ran home faster than he had ever gone
before.

*   *   *

It was a strange world to live in, where men were
full of fears and superstition, where the Church
made money and held power because of people's
ignorance. At the same time, it was an exciting
world, for men were discovering new knowledge
and new lands. While Martin was still at school,
Columbus discovered the West Indian Islands and
his fellow-explorers went on to prove that the earth
was completely round, and not flat as most people
had always believed. Martin learned easily and
quickly, taking in the old knowledge and feeling
the thrill of what was new. From school, he went on
to the university at Erfurt, matriculating and
gaining his B.A. and then his M.A.

Night after night, when the day's studies were
over, he took his lute and sat with his student
friends in an Erfurt inn or, in the summer time,
under the trees, playing the songs he had been
taught as a boy, rolling out the lovely German
words instead of the Latin he had been using all
day. His friends smiled as he played, and then
patted him on the back, telling him he was even
better with his lute than he was with his books.

His father would never have believed that
Back in Eisenach, where they now lived, Hans
Luther boasted about his brilliant son. "A fine
young man, Martin is," he told all who would

sten. "A scholar! His professors say he's the best
1 the whole university. Why, when he comes
ome even *I* call him 'sir', you know!" He nodded
is head proudly. "Aye—he'll go a long way, will
1y son Martin. Become one of the greatest
awyers in Erfurt, I shouldn't wonder. Why, he
1ight be known all over Germany!" Hans nodded
gain, knowingly, and picked up his pewter
ankard of ale. Neither Hans nor Martin, nor any
f his friends, guessed that he would become one of
he best known names in the world.

2

THE THUNDERSTORM

OVERHEAD, the sky was a deep grey, though towards Stotternheim the clouds were almost black. The air was heavy, and the horse was covered with sweat as its rider urged it on towards the distant town. In the stillness of the hot, sultry July afternoon the young horseman seemed to be the only moving creature in the landscape. He wiped the perspiration off his forehead and thrust his long hair back over his head.

"I don't like it," he muttered to himself. "I feel as if something dreadful is going to happen . . . almost as if the world was coming to an end!"

Martin Luther was twenty-one, and he was returning to the university at Erfurt after spending a brief holiday with his parents. His father had made him feel awkward by introducing him to the neighbours as "Doctor Martin", which he was not, and pleased him by a lovely present of a valuable book about the law. In the little town of Eisenach, where his father still worked as hard as ever in his foundries, Martin was already a distinguished young man. Other people, as well as his father, knew that he was one of the cleverest students at the university, and most of them said the same thing. "He'll be making a lot of money soon, will Master Martin, and then poor old Hans and Margarita will be able to sit back and take life easily. They've had to go without a lot of things to give that boy such a good education! Now that he's on his way to being a wealthy lawyer he'll be able to pay them back a bit, and look after them!"

Even when he was at home, however, Martin showed that he was not quite like other men, for, when there was a party and all the company were gaily drinking and singing songs, someone would call on him to play the lute, only to find that he was no longer there. Instead, he was somewhere outside the town, walking by himself. His parents would shrug their shoulders helplessly. "He's in one of his moods again!" they would say. "Better let him walk it off!" In those moods he was poor company indeed, as his university friends knew. They had come more often lately, too, and lasted longer. Martin himself could hardly have explained them. He felt that in spite of all his hard work, his regular attendance at church services and his private prayers, God was angry with him. If the end of the world were to come suddenly, or if he were to die, he would certainly be sent to Hell. In these despairing hours he was terrified of God, of Jesus, even of the Virgin Mary whom he usually loved. The only safe place, he felt, would be in a monastery, for even at the end of the world monks would always be judged more kindly than other people, since they spent so much of their time praying and going to church. Then he would start arguing with himself again. He did not want to be a monk. He wanted to be a lawyer, famous and rich, helping his parents and enjoying the good things of the world.

*   *   *

Now that the holiday was over and he was on his way back to Erfurt these thoughts had been in his mind once more. At the moment, however, he had forgotten them. All he wanted to do was to get to some place—a cottage or a shepherd's hut, if he could not reach town—before the storm overtook him and he was soaked to the skin. In the distance the black clouds grew thicker and a heavy, cold spot of rain struck against his hand. The dark sky was split by a brilliant flash of lightning that lit up the whole countryside. The horse jerked at the reins anxiously and then jumped in terror, nearly throwing its rider off, as a gigantic peal of thunder rolled out. Martin tightened the reins in his hand, gripped the animal's flanks firmly with his knees and urged it forward. There came another flash which seemed to strike the ground a hundred yards away and then, as the thunder pealed out, another more brilliant than the rest which almost blinded Martin. He felt as if he had been hit. His whole body shook as the lightning struck him and he crashed off his horse on to the roadway, covering his eyes in terror.

"St. Anne, help me!" His voice, crying to the patron saint of his mining family, rang out across the countryside. "St. Anne, save me! I promise to become a monk!"

The storm passed. Wet through to the skin, Martin crawled to his feet, staggered on till he found his horse again and clambered into the saddle. He had made his promise and now nothing would ever be able to change it. Whatever his friends said, however his father argued, he was finished with the law. The mother of the Virgin Mary had saved him from God's anger and from dying in the storm. He must keep his promise. He must become a monk.

At the farewell party which he gave to his student friends they were amazed, though they knew better than to try and stop anyone from fulfilling a vow of this kind. They drank and sang merrily enough while Martin told them of his plans. He had chosen one of the strictest monasteries in Erfurt—the Augustinian convent. He would have no money, no clothes of his own except the monk's gown and hood. He would always have to do what he was told and go where he was sent. He would have little to eat at the best of times and would often have to fast, going without food for three or four days at a time. His friends shook their heads sadly. It was so very unlike all they had thought Martin was going to achieve.

From the party Luther went straight to the monastery gates, standing outside with a few friends. He had already made arrangements to be admitted as a novice, or learner, and when he knocked a quiet old man opened the door and, without a word, motioned him inside. Martin said a word of farewell, passed beyond the wall and heard the gate close behind him. It was all done. He had finished with the world outside. From this day onwards, he would be able to find peace in the quietness of the monastery.

Standing on the altar steps the prior of the monastery looked down on the thick-set young man below him. The monks were all poor men, but the church itself was bright and gay. Gold and gilt reflected the sunlight, which lit up the brilliant colours of the altar cloths and the gaudily-painted images of the saints round the walls. Martin saw nothing of all this. His eyes were on the man who would now be the most important person in his life. The prior motioned with his hand, and Martin sank to his knees at the foot of the steps.

"What do you want?"

Martin replied that he wished to please God.

"Are you married? In debt? Ill?"

He answered each question in turn and the prior went on to describe the harshness of life in the monastery—little food, rough clothing, begging in the town, prayers throughout the night, not much sleep, no wife, no children, no home of his own. Was he prepared for all this?

"Yes." Martin nodded, a look of hope in his face.
"Yes, with God's help."

The choir began to chant. His hair was clipped
and then his head was shaved. He felt his own
bright student's clothes stripped off and the rough,
monk's clothing thrown about his body. Someone
whispered to him and he lay down on the floor of
the church before the altar, stretching out his arms
in the form of a cross. When the choir finished singing the prior moved down from the steps, lifted him
to his feet, clasped his hands between his own for a
moment and passed down the church. The other
monks passed by in a line, unsmiling, without a
word, doing the same thing. The last man passed
by and, in the silence of the monastery church,
Martin stood alone. He looked round, felt the
rough cloth as his arms dropped to his sides, and
smiled with content. Everything would be easy,
now. He was a monk.

*   *   *

As a matter of fact, he was not fully admitted
as a monk until a year later. Those first twelve
months were a time of trial. The prior could have
refused to keep him or Martin might have changed
his mind. Nothing of the kind happened. He loved
the prayers in his own tiny stone cell and the seven
services which he attended in the chapel each day.
He did not mind fasting even for three or four
days at a time, and thought himself privileged

when he was given a sack, day after day, and told
to go out into the town and beg bread for the
monastery.

Two years after he entered his new life he was to
celebrate Mass for the first time in the chapel.
Word had been sent to his father, so that the family
might come for the great occasion, and, early in the
morning, with twenty other horsemen, old Hans
Luther rode into the courtyard of the monastery.
Father and son did not meet before the service, for
Martin had to spend longer than usual in prayer
that morning, and the first Hans saw of him was
when he came in and stood in front of the altar,
clothed in the bright robes of the priest. At one
point in the service Martin hesitated, gripping the
altar as if he were going to fall. He said afterwards
that God had seemed so near, and he still thought
of himself as such a sinful man, that he did not
dare go on. The congregation watched him,
frightened in case he fainted, but after a moment
he straightened up and went on. When he came
afterwards to join his father and his guests at the
table where they were eating he was still white and
trembling.

Perhaps it was because the father wondered if,
after all, his son was well and happy, that Hans
looked up a little angrily. It was the first time they
had met for two years, and the old man had still
not got over all his anger about Martin's change of
plans.

"I suppose you still think you've done the right thing, eh?" he growled. "It's all right being a monk or a priest, my lad—but your mother and I thought you were going to be famous!"

"I have no wish to be famous." Martin's voice was milder than it used to be. He had learned in the monastery that one does not argue.

The old man looked sharply at him. "Famous men earn good money. We were expecting a bit of *that*, too, after all we've spent on you!"

Martin would have replied angrily a couple of years earlier. Now he merely said: "I can do more good by praying for you than giving you money."

Hans Luther snorted. "Prayers don't buy food and firewood, my lad."

Martin's reply should have settled the argument, but it did not. "I was called by a voice from heaven. God spoke to me in the thunderstorm."

"Well," answered his father, thoughtfully, "I hope you're right. I've seen a lot of monks in my time, I have, and I can't say they all look as happy as you seem to be. Come on, lad, eat up; you look half-starved."

Martin picked up a chunk of dry bread. "Right, father? Of course I'm right. The Church has accepted me, and the Church is always right."

He was not going to be quite so sure of that in three years' time.

3

THE HOLY CITY

LIKE all Christians of his time, Martin believed that though bad people were sent to Hell and good ones eventually went to Heaven, almost everyone, when they died, went to Purgatory. This was a place of torture, where men were made to suffer for their sins. A soul might have to stay in Purgatory for tens of thousands of years until at last it was fit for Heaven. Fortunately, people believed, there were ways of shortening this long period of suffering. Friends could pay priests to say Mass for those who died—that is, hold special services—and the more Masses that were said the quicker the period in Purgatory would end. Another way was to visit and look at the many thousands of holy objects, known as relics. Sometimes this might involve a very long pilgrimage, but that was all the better in the end because even more years were taken off the time in Purgatory. However strange much of this may appear, it is easy to understand that people who believed in goblins and witches did not find it hard to believe in the things that the Church taught about pilgrimages and holy relics. There were more relics in Rome than any other city in the world, and so, from Britain and Ireland, from Spain to the Northlands, men and women constantly made their pilgrimage to the Holy City.

Martin himself often wished he could join the pilgrims. His first years in the monastery at Erfurt had been calm and happy, but as the months went by he found he was growing uneasy. He was sure that God was still angry with him, and certain that he must have done wrong things for which he had not been forgiven. Perhaps if he could go to Rome he would have time to see all the relics and gain God's forgiveness in that way. It was all the more surprising, therefore, when the prior of the monastery sent for him one day. He entered the prior's room with another monk who had also been summoned.

"Brother Martin," said the prior, quietly, "I am going to send you—both of you—on a journey." Martin would have liked to look at the other monk, but he knew he must keep his eyes cast down while the prior spoke to him. "There is a gathering of all the Augustinian monasteries to which we must send representatives. Two must go from Erfurt. I have chosen you."

Martin looked up now. "Where must we go?"

"To Rome." The answer was so unexpected that he could not help looking at his friend. He found the same look of joy on his face that he knew must be on his own. "It is a long journey. You will have to walk all the way, begging your food as you go. You will spend a month in Rome and then return. I will tell you more before you set out." As they left the room he almost wished he were a university student again, so that he could run along the corridor, singing at the top of his voice. Instead, he was a young monk, who must walk slowly with his hands together, just as though he had not heard the most wonderful news in the world.

*   *   *

It was indeed a long journey, which took them through countries where they could not understand the language and were glad that they spoke Latin so well. They passed lovely lakes, thick forests and over the snowy passes of the Alps before they reached the hot, flat plains of Northern Italy, wondering if they would ever reach Rome at all. Then, one day, as the sun was high in the sky, they caught the gleam of light in the distance. The sun was shining on the Holy City. Martin and his brother-monk stopped at once, as did all the pilgrims whom they had joined on the road. He pointed ahead, and found that others had seen it, too. There was an air of excitement in the crowd.

"Hail, Holy Rome!"

The phrase was murmured again and again, as it had been by every pilgrim for hundreds of years on the first sight of the great city. With new energy the whole company surged forward along the road which grew busier with travellers, carts and soldiers as they drew nearer to the end of their journey.

Martin would never have believed that he would have been disappointed with the Holy City, the home of the Pope, the place from which the Church was ruled. Yet, from the very first day he spent in Rome, he felt both sad and angry. He was not interested in the wonderful new paintings that the great artists were doing in the Roman chapels, though long afterwards they would be regarded as some of the city's greatest treasures. He did not even bother to stare at the ruins of the Colosseum or the statues of the gods and goddesses of ancient Rome. He cared only about the Church, and that was where he was most disappointed.

He found that Roman priests could say five or six Masses while he was taking just one service. They gabbled through the words he loved as if they meant nothing at all. When he tried to talk to some of them, in their rich robes, they stared at the simple monk who spoke Latin with a heavy German accent, and laughed.

"You don't *believe* in all this nonsense of relics and masses, do you?" they asked, shrugging their shoulders.

*   *   *

He had made up his mind to worship in every church in Rome, and that was not easy, with the other services he had to attend in the monastery where he was staying, even though he had a month in the city. There were so many churches and shrines that he lost count of them. The number of holy relics in the city no one had ever tried to count. One church claimed that seventy thousand martyrs from the days of the Roman persecutions were buried in its crypt. Another claimed to have one of the coins paid to Judas when he betrayed Jesus, and beside one of the city gateways were white marks which the guides said were left by stones which had turned to snowballs when angry crowds flung them at St. Paul fourteen hundred years earlier. Martin found himself wondering whether he was really doing much good after all by visiting all the relics in Rome. He tried to add up all the hundreds of years he had saved himself in Purgatory by his pilgrimage in the city and found he had quite lost count.

One day he went to see the foundations which were being laid for the new cathedral, St. Peter's, which would be the most wonderful church in the world. It looked tremendous, and he wondered where they would find the money to build it. He said as much to a prosperous-looking priest standing beside him. The Italian laughed, and chinked a bag of gold by his side. "We'll get it, all right," he answered. "It will come out of the pockets of people all over Europe who believe the Pope is a godly man and they must do everything he tells them!"

"The Pope? But he *is* a godly man!" replied Martin. "He is the head of the Church!"

The Italian priest smiled. "You beg for your food, I suppose?" he asked. "And live in poverty in a tiny stone room? I wonder how *he* would like to live in coarse robes like yours!" He pointed to a litter which was being carried through the wide square. The men who bore it wore rich clothes. Soldiers walked ahead of it and behind it. The man who sat there, sheltered from the sun by a canopy of cloth-of-gold, waved his hand languidly in blessing over the crowd. Huge rings glittered on it. His face was sulky and he looked like some pampered prince or duke.

"Who is that?" asked Martin, in astonishment.

"Get down on your knees, my foolish friend," replied the Italian. "*That* is His Holiness the Pope!"

The worst moment of all was when Martin trudged towards the marble stairs to which all pilgrims went when they visited Rome. They were known as the *Scala Sancta*, and were supposed to be the very stairs on which Jesus had stood outside Pilate's palace in Jerusalem. Pilgrims began at the bottom and climbed upwards on their knees, pausing to kiss each step and say the Lord's Prayer as they did so. To do this meant that the pilgrim could release the soul of some friend from Purgatory and get him into Heaven at once. The first thing that Martin noticed was that none of the Italian priests or monks was climbing the stairs. The Romans themselves evidently did not believe

very firmly in what the Church said. Then, as h
moved upwards, kissing each step, saying hi
prayers each time, he thought again of the thous
ands of relics he had seen, the scores of churche
he had visited, in the city. He shook his head an
tried to get the thoughts that troubled him out o
his mind. But, at the top, he rose slowly to his feet

"I wonder," he murmured. "I wonder if it's al
as true as they say!"

*   *   *

When the month was over Martin trudge
slowly back across Europe to his monastery i
Erfurt. It was a very different journey from the on
in the other direction. Then he had been full o
excitement at the thought of seeing Rome an
worshipping in its many churches, perhaps eve
seeing the Pope himself. Now, he was full o
doubts. The things he, and every boy in Europe
was taught might all be wrong. God might still b
angry with him because of his sins, and if God too
no notice of pilgrimages and visits to the shrine
with their holy relics, how could he ever hope to b
forgiven or get to Heaven? He tramped slowly an
sadly along the roads leading to Germany. H
would have to talk to the prior of the monaster
in Erfurt about it when he got home—but some
how he did not think it would be much help i
his despair.

Meanwhile, as Martin was walking home fron

Rome, one of the great rulers of Germany was planning something which was going to change the whole of Martin Luther's life and, in the end, the history of the world. In the tiny town of Witten-berg, a hundred miles or so from Erfurt, Duke Frederick the Wise paced up and down the hall of his castle. Every now and again he paused to look through the open window towards the new buildings which were being added to the Witten-berg university, of which he was so proud. His face was troubled, and he swung round quickly when the door of the hall opened and a monk entered.

"Ah, von Staupitz," he cried, advancing towards him, his silk cloak billowing out behind him. "I'm glad you've come so soon." He turned and waved his hand towards the window. "The university is coming on well. We shall be as famous as Leipzig after all!"

"I hope so, my lord," replied Staupitz, quietly. "But if that's to be so, we shall need more pro-fessors than we have now. Better ones, too!"

"We shan't get any better than you, Johann. Why, it's because you teach so well about the Bible that students are already coming in bigger numbers. But you're right—we've got to have more professors. Younger men, too, whom the students will like and respect. We need at least three."

Staupitz, the leader of the Augustinian monastery in Wittenberg, nodded. "I don't know about three, my lord Duke, but there is *one* man I have in mind. He might have been a great lawyer if he hadn't become a monk. I think he'd make a fine professor for your university—young Luther, from Erfurt."

4

MARTIN DISCOVERS THE BIBLE

"NOT much of it, is there?" said Martin, pulling a wry face as he gazed at the village clustered under the shelter of the low, white, sandy hill. He could see the castle at one end of the village and the church, surrounded by grey monastery buildings, at the other. Between them, with less than a mile separating the cottages at one end from those at the other, stretched the rickety, steep-roofed houses that made up the town of Wittenberg.

"Well," replied the man who had walked the last few miles with him, "it's not so big as Erfurt, certainly. But you'd better not let any Wittenberger hear you say anything against it. They're as proud of their city as if it were Rome itself. They've got plenty of clever men there, brother; and there isn't a better prince in the whole of Germany than Duke Frederick. Everybody knows him—you can tell that from the size of the town—and everybody loves him."

Martin nodded without comment. He could see the silver of the river Elbe as it flowed towards the town, passing by on the further side, and now the

c

wide moat that defended the nearer side was plain, too. Yes, he thought to himself, a year or two here would perhaps be a pleasant change from the busy life of Erfurt. He looked at his companion, taking a new interest in what he was saying. If the man had told him that this was the place where he was going to spend all the rest of his life he would have thought he was talking nonsense, though it was true enough.

"A fine collection of relics the Duke has collected in Wittenberg, they say."

"Indeed?" Martin looked a little doubtful, thinking of what he had seen in Rome.

"Aye. Sent all over the world for them, he has. Paid no end of money, and given away half his jewels to buy them, so they say. Wonderful they are, too. There's a straw from the manger where Jesus was born. And a piece of the stone where He stood when He ascended into Heaven." The man's voice was growing more excited. "There's even a twig from the burning bush that Moses saw all those thousands of years ago."

Martin did not reply directly. "This Duke Frederick must be a very rich man," he answered instead. "Spending all that money and still being able to build a university and keep it going."

"Ah, but that's the point. Don't you see? He keeps the university going, pays his professors and so on, out of the money people pay to see the straw and the burning bush and the saints' bones and so on!" The man laughed. "No wonder they call him Frederick the Wise!"

*   *   *

Martin was twenty-eight when he took up his duties at Wittenberg. From the beginning he liked Duke Frederick and Johann von Staupitz, the head of the monastery who taught the university students about the Bible. They liked him, too, and felt they had been right to bring him to Wittenberg. One day, they were sure, he would be famous enough to draw students from all over Germany. Even after he had been there only a few months, people turned to look at him as he walked down the narrow main street, where the water ran down the centre in an open drain from the river at one end to the water-mill at the other. Women throwing their slops into the drain, men sitting in the inns and students with their books under their arms and a lute over their shoulders would nudge one another. "That's the new professor," they would murmur. "Clever fellow, they say, and a very holy one, too. Spends no end of time at his prayers. But I can't say he looks very happy, all the same!"

That, unfortunately, was true. Indeed, Martin was more unhappy than ever. He would pray for hours on end, walk round the church and look at the images of the saints or the caskets where the holy relics were kept, lie on the floor of his cell for eight hours at a time wearing hardly any clothes so that the cold would keep him awake while he gazed at the crucifix on the wall. None of it seemed to help. God was still very far off, and when he had done everything he could think of to make amends for his sins he was sure that God was still angry with him. He grew thin with worry, and his eyes became sunken and dull. The Duke asked Staupitz what was the matter with him, and the vicar of the monastery called Martin into his room.

"The trouble with you, Brother Martin, is that you make religion too difficult. Why should you think that God is always angry with you? He loves you—and all you have to do is to love Him, too."

The advice was no use, and Staupitz went on wondering how he could help the unhappy monk. Perhaps he needed more work to take his mind off his worries, he thought. One morning he saw Martin walking slowly to and fro in the monastery garden and, making up his mind, went out to talk to him again.

"Brother Martin," he called. Luther stopped, almost under the pear tree that stood in the garden, and the elderly monk came up to him. "I've got some news for you. I think it's time I slacked off a bit with some of my lecturing. There are a great many other duties I ought to attend to, and I haven't time." As Martin stared at him in surprise, the older man went on. "I'm going to give up being the professor of Bible studies."

"But . . . but . . ." Martin stammered, "it's because of *you* that men come to the university. You can't do that, sir. Whoever could take your place?"

Staupitz paused for a moment or two, gazing at Martin. "*You* will, Brother Martin. It will mean a lot of hard work, I'm afraid, but you're the very man for the job."

Martin looked horrified. "But I don't *know* much about the Bible."

"Then it's time you did," said Staupitz, and walked away, leaving Martin staring unbelievingly after him.

It was very true. Like most monks and priests of his time, Martin had learned a great deal about the Church and its worship, he knew something about law, he could recite the life-stories of dozens of saints, and had read scores of books, copied out by hand in the libraries of the monastery, but he had read very little of the Bible itself. Ordinary people, of course, who could not understand the Latin in which it was written and read in Church, had never read it at all. Martin walked slowly into the reading-room of the monastery, searched along the shelves until he came to the great vellum volumes which contained the Bible, and began to look through them. There were parts that he had never opened at all. He took one of the volumes down, laid it on the wooden table, sat down on the rough form and began to read.

* * *

Staupitz's appointment of Luther as professor of the Bible had some startling results, almost at once. The first was that Martin found the Bible much more interesting than he had ever imagined. The next was that the more he read of it, the more sure he became that God was not really angry with him after all. The Bible said that if you loved God, and believed Him—"had faith in Him", was the way the Bible put it—there was nothing that need worry you. Curiously enough, there was nothing in the Bible about saying your prayers for hours on end, or worshipping the saints, or asking the priest to forgive you after you had confessed to him. There was nothing in it about going on pilgrimages, or paying money to see the saints' relics or holy bones. All it said was that God loved you, that Jesus died to show you that God really *did* love you, and that you had to believe that these things were true.

Martin wondered why he had been so long in finding this out. Then, to his astonishment, he discovered that his doubts had disappeared. God *had* forgiven him, and he was quite sure of it. This was something he would have to tell everyone he met—and the first people who must be told were the students he was appointed to teach.

The classrooms where Martin taught grew more and more crowded as the weeks passed. Day by day Martin walked into the lecture hall with a big volume under his arm. In the beginning it was the book of Psalms, then it was Paul's letter to the Romans, and later on Paul's letter to the Galatians.

Instead of rambling on in dull Latin that made students want to go to sleep, he read them what the Bible said and then explained it as he saw it, always coming back to the point that what mattered was knowing God for yourself, as someone near and fatherly, not far-off like a king or a judge. Every now and again he dropped into using some everyday German phrase to make his meaning more clear.

Sometimes students would ask questions or make comments, and Martin often found himself biting his tongue before he answered. A student would say: "But, Doctor Martin, the Church has always taught that you should pray to the saints," or "Doctor Luther, the Church says that you are forgiven because you go on pilgrimages and worship at a place where the body of a saint has been buried!" There was one answer Martin felt he ought to give, but it would have been a very dangerous thing to say.

"Then the teaching of the Church is wrong! Even the Pope himself is wrong if he says what is not in the Bible!" That was what he *felt* like saying, but it would have taken more courage than he possessed just then. People who said such things were turned out of the Church. They might be imprisoned or even killed. Perhaps the time would come when he would have to say it, but for the moment he simply taught what he read in the Bible about God being One who loved and forgave us, even without priests or penance. Besides, he had not had time to think it all out in his own mind, for there were so many other things to be done.

He preached in the monastery church and in the Duke's parish church. He made lists of studies for the new students, and interviewed them when they were slacking or needed advice. He superintended the fish-pond in the monastery grounds, making sure that there were enough fish to last them for Friday meals throughout the year. He had to visit and oversee eleven other monasteries in the district. When he should have been going to bed he sat up writing endless letters. He was so full of work that, instead of saying his prayers every day, he saved them up on one occasion for three weeks, and then spent a whole Sunday reading through the prayers he should have recited each day.

He might have gone on like that for years if one of the students had not come to him after his lectures one morning and said something that made him think hard. "They say that monk Tetzel, is going all over Germany, Doctor Luther.

What do you think of him and these pardons he's selling to everybody? If you're right, Doctor, *he's* wrong. And that means the *Church* is wrong! What do you think about that?"

5

THE MAN WHO SOLD FORGIVENESS

THERE was an air of excitement throughout the whole town. Boys and girls crowded round the city gate, shop-keepers set out their most attractive wares to catch the eyes of passers-by, monks and priests bustled to and fro, pausing to chatter in their deep, German voices before they went on their way again. In the market-place soldiers paraded, keeping the bystanders away from the centre, where the old town-cross stood, with their long pikes and lances. Suddenly, the raucous blare of trumpets cut through the babble of the crowds.

"It's him! It's the monk, Tetzel!" From the wooden houses, down the narrow lanes, the towns-people poured towards the high street leading to the market square. Along it came a procession. A group of soldiers walked first, in the glittering uniform which showed that they came from the household of the Archbishop of Mainz. Behind them walked the trumpeters, silent now that they were in the city. Then came the mayor and the chief men of the city in their red robes, the golden chains of office jangling around their shoulders. Behind them a monk carried a silk cushion, with a single roll of parchment laid on it, and another monk bore a tall cross with the coat-of-arms of the Pope in the centre. Then, at last, the man all the people were anxious to see—Tetzel, the monk who would sell them forgiveness for their sins.

Slowly the procession moved forward to the market. The Pope's cross was set up, the mayor made a speech welcoming the monk, and then the people pushed past the soldiers to listen. Just in case the whole town did not know he was there, Tetzel made a sign to the trumpeters, who blew another blast, and to the drummers by their side, who went on banging at their drums until he put up his hand for silence. Then he began to speak.

It was an unpleasant sermon, all about the tortures people suffered in Purgatory. Those who listened shivered and shuddered, and little children hid their heads in their mothers' aprons. When his listeners felt that they could not bear to listen to another word, the monk asked a question. "How much would you pay to escape from tortures like this and get straight into Heaven?" Then he asked another. "How much would you pay to get your friends out of Purgatory and get *them* into Heaven?" At that moment the people who had been listening felt they would pay almost anything, and they pressed forward with their hands plunged into their leather purses which were tied to their belts, but it was not as easy as that.

"His Holiness the Pope has promised forgiveness to those who will buy it. He says so in this letter." He pointed to the parchment roll on the cushion. Then he called up one of the monks who were with him. "Here are copies of the Pope's letter of forgiveness!" The assistant brought out a great handful of pieces of paper. "They cost a lot of money, but they're worth the price. Who wants to buy forgiveness for his sins?" As the money was stretched out to him in grimy, hard-working hands, he held up his own and pushed them away. "It costs kings and queens—and bishops!— twenty-five golden florins." There was a gasp from the people. "Merchants have only to pay three. And you poor people need only pay one golden florin!"

Poor peasants had to work a long time before they saw a golden florin, but they knew the monk was coming and they had brought out their savings. Gold coins gleamed in the air, tumbled into Tetzel's outstretched hands, rolled on to the stone flags of the market-place. On the outskirts of the crowd men and women clamoured to push their way in, fearing that all the "indulgences" would be sold before they could reach the monk. They need not have worried. There were enough letters for everyone, and plenty to spare for the next town they came to, as well.

Not many of them asked where the·money was going, but Martin Luther knew well enough what would happen to it. He remembered the foundations of St. Peter's Cathedral in Rome. Grass had been growing amongst them and there were weeds sprouting from the walls because there was not enough money to pay the builders. The work had stopped until the old Pope died and a new one was elected. The new one had ideas of his own. People would always pay money to be forgiven, and he agreed to a scheme by which "indulgences"—letters of "forgiveness"—should be sold for high prices. The money raised would come to Rome to help to build St. Peter's.

* * *

In Wittenberg, townspeople crowded round Martin Luther as he went to preach in the parish church. Tetzel had not yet visited Wittenberg, but many of them had been to hear him in other towns. They thrust their letters out to Martin and asked him to read them. "Forgiveness for myself, for everything I've done," said one man.

"I've got my mother and father out of Purgatory," cried a merchant, "but it cost me a lot of money!"

Another cheerful, red-faced man laughed. "Look at this," he cried. "My letter says I've paid for forgiveness for all the wrong things I do between now and the time I die!"

A grumbling voice cut in. "It's all very well, but I don't like it. All this good German gold going to

Italy to build a church at Rome. It doesn't seem right to me! Why can't we keep our money in our own country and build churches here instead?"

Martin's face was gloomy as he walked slowly up the aisle to begin the service. Those who listened knew that he was not really thinking about what he was saying. He elbowed his way almost roughly past those who stood at the door waiting to talk to him as he came out of church and marched up to the castle, ready for an appointment which he had made with his patron, Duke Frederick the Wise.

In the stone hall of the castle, with its walls hung with bright tapestries, the Duke sat forward as Martin walked into the room. He was a heavy man, with a thick grey beard, which he stroked now and again as he talked.

"This monk Tetzel . . ." began Martin.

"It's all right, Doctor Martin," put in the Duke, quickly. "I've heard all about him. I don't like the sound of him."

"Nor I, my lord. If he comes to Wittenberg I shall have to tell my people not to listen to him or to buy his indulgences."

"You needn't worry, friend. Tetzel isn't coming to Wittenberg. I've told the Archbishop that I won't have him here. If he comes I shall turn him out. *I'm* the Duke here, and I'll have no preachers that I don't agree with!"

Martin smiled for the first time that day.

"Good!" he said. "I'm glad to hear it, my lord!"
The Duke's next words made his smile fade.

"I'm not a fool, Dr. Martin. Where does the
money come from for the university? To pay you
and the rest of the professors? Eh? You know
well enough. It comes from my own great collection of holy relics . . . five thousand of them, Dr.
Martin . . . the biggest collection in Germany, so
they say. On All Saints' Day they'll be set out in
the castle church and people will come in hundreds
to see them. They'll pay good money, too."

"What for?"

The Duke looked angrily at him. "What do you
mean, what for? You know as well as I do. They'll
pay to see the things in the church, and touch
the caskets they're kept in, because by doing that
they'll get their sins forgiven." He snorted
furiously, and stood up to stump round the hall.
"Tetzel, indeed! Let some monk come here and
take my townspeople's money to build a Roman
church when I need it myself to keep my university going! Rubbish! Don't you worry about
Tetzel or anybody like him, my friend. *I'll* deal
with *him!* Now, off you go and get on with your
lecturing, Herr Professor. I've got other things to
think about besides monks."

Martin walked slowly back to his cell in the
monastery. That was not how he thought now.
Tetzel was wrong, the Duke was wrong, the
Pope was wrong. The Church was wrong. What-

ever happened, he would have to say what he thought. There was not long to make up his mind what to do, but already he had a plan which he thought would set things moving. Back in his room he got a piece of parchment and began to write, scratching words out and rewriting whole sentences, numbering them down the side. One, two, three, four. The writing went on, and the numbers rose to thirty, forty, fifty. Out to the monastery services, back to his cell, out to his lectures, back to his cell to go on writing came the angry monk. He knew now that if he went on there would be trouble, but if he did not, he would never have a clear conscience as long as he lived.

*　　*　　*

Pilgrims crowded into the little town as All Saints' Day drew near. They walked by the river, sat by the moat outside the walls, gaped at the Duke's castle and waited outside the gate for a glimpse of the Duke himself. Many of them, however, were even more anxious to see the professor who was supposed to be the greatest man in Wittenberg. Perhaps, they thought, Dr. Luther would explain the relics to them when they were set out in the castle church on the first day in November. Certainly they would hear him preach about them.

It was in the afternoon of All Saints' Eve that Martin walked slowly out of the monastery towards the parish church of Wittenberg. He carried a big sheet of paper in his hand, and a hammer stuck out of the pocket of his monk's robe. At the main door of the church he stopped, pulled out the hammer and a handful of nails and began to fasten the paper to the door. The sound of the hammer-blows echoed inside the church, and interested spectators came running up from the street to see what was happening. Over the monk's shoulder, as he stood for a moment to look at what he had nailed up, the onlookers saw a long list of numbered sentences. Martin said nothing, going back through the crowd with a grim look on his face. Come what may, he had done what he knew was right.

Behind him, a great buzz of excitement broke out, and people called to one another to come and read the paper. There were ninety-five paragraphs on it, some very short, some much longer. Some of them the readers could not understand at all, but others were clear enough. Slowly a strange silence fell in front of the church door as ordinary people, monks, the Duke's servants, went on reading.

"Martin Luther says that indulgences are wrong . . . he says it's no use paying money to see holy relics . . . God does not forgive men for reasons like that . . . Martin Luther says . . . Martin Luther says. . . ." The people went on reading, skipping what they could not understand. By the time they had finished, two things were very clear.

Martin Luther, the monk of Wittenberg, said that a great many of the things the Church and the Pope did were wrong. And whether Martin was right himself, or wrong, there was trouble for him ahead.

6

"LUTHER MUST BE BURNED!"

MARTIN took the letter and looked at it carefully. His hand was quite still and the thick paper never even trembled, although he knew that what was written here might very well be his death-sentence. He looked up at his friend, Staupitz, and nodded.

"You're quite right. It is an order from the Pope himself. I am to go to Rome within two months, to be tried by the Church."

"If you do, they'll burn you, Brother Martin!"

Martin dropped the parchment on the table. "That's why I'm not going, Staupitz."

"You'll disobey the Pope himself?"

"I've disobeyed him already, friend, by what I nailed on the church door. I've said he is wrong in many of the things that he teaches. You agree with me; and so do many people in Wittenberg, and others outside of here. He says I am not to preach."

"So?"

"So I shall preach in spite of him." He turned swiftly to his friend. "You know, I owe you a lot, Johann. It was you who brought me to Wittenberg. And this is about the only State in Germany where

51

I could remain in safety. Every other prince is anxious to stand well with the Emperor or the Pope, to have more land given him from the one or more honours from the other. Only Duke Frederick, amongst the lot of them, is really anxious to do what is right." He stumped up and down the room, his voice ringing round it. "And he *is*, you know. He's not sure whether I'm right or wrong, but he rather *thinks* I'm right. And you see what that means, don't you, Johann? He will have to stand out against the Pope, and his representatives here in Germany. He'll have to give up his relics and the money he gets from them. I don't like putting him in a hole like that, Johann."

Staupitz smiled gently. "Then perhaps you'd better go to Rome after all."

The sound of Martin's cheerful laugh rang through the narrow windows. "And be burned? Oh no! I sent a message to Duke Frederick telling him I would willingly go to Switzerland or France so that he would be free of me, but he won't have it. He's trying to get my trial transferred from Rome to Germany, and he insists that he'll stand by me and see that I'm kept safe, however loudly the cardinals and the Pope shout that I should be burned."

*   *   *

The months that followed were very crowded for Martin. He was still the busiest man in the university. "I shall be busier than ever today," he

"LUTHER MUST BE BURNED!" 53

once wrote, "so I shall have to spend even more time praying." That seemed a strange way of getting through the day, but those who saw Martin's cheerful face and heard him lecturing knew that God was very real to him indeed. He was never too busy to talk to God, and to listen to what God had to say to him. That was why he could still be gay, even when most of his friends dreaded what was going to happen to him.

It was almost exactly a year after Martin had nailed the paper to the Wittenberg church door that the Pope's special messenger, Cardinal Cajetan, came to the famous town of Augsburg. He had to try and win recruits for another crusade against the Turks; he had to raise money from Germany to pay the armies who were to fight the Turks; he had to try and persuade Martin Luther that the opinions he held were wrong. He made large presents to the dukes who had come to talk over affairs, and to the bishops and archbishops whose support he wanted. In the middle of the "Diet", as the gathering was called, Martin arrived from Wittenberg, his heavy monk's robes hanging loosely on his thin body.

The cardinal in his bright scarlet robes and red hat looked at Martin next day as he entered the council chamber. It should have been easy to prove him wrong. After all, he was only an ordinary monk, and it was his duty to believe what the cardinal, the Pope's representative, would tell him. The cardinal was not very optimistic. Everything had gone wrong with his mission so far, and he could not believe that Martin's case would be very easy, either. The dukes and bishops had taken his presents, and then refused to raise money or provide men to fight the Turks. Too much money went out of Germany already, they said bluntly, to support a Pope in an Italian palace and build an Italian cathedral. They would give no more. It was time some German or other had the courage to stand up for his own country, even if it did mean defying the cardinal and the Pope. The cardinal smoothed a crease out of the scarlet silk as he rose to look down on Martin.

"I have called you to Augsburg, Doctor Luther, so that you may say publicly that you have been wrong in your opinions and your statements."

Martin took a step forward. "But I can prove from the Bible . . ." he began.

The cardinal held up his hand, and the broad sleeve dropped away from his arm, its deeper lining gleaming for a moment in the autumn sunlight. He looked more like a prince than a priest. "You will prove nothing, Doctor Luther. I am forbidden to *argue* with you; I am here only to hear you admit that you were wrong." He pointed to the stone floor. "Have you forgotten to whom you speak?"

For a second or two the room was still, then Martin took a pace back, knelt and finally bowed

down in front of the cardinal with his head on the
stone floor. It was the proper way for a monk
to salute the Pope's messenger. With a gentle
smile, the cardinal bent down and lifted him up.
He thought, after all, it might not be so difficult as
he had feared. He might take the monk to Rome,
and win promotion for himself by ridding the
Church of one of its most dangerous figures.

*   *   *

How wrong he was, he discovered next day.
Martin insisted that he was right in all he had said.
If the Bible was right, then the teachers of the
Church were wrong. Cajetan's mouth was drawn
into a thin line and his face was grim as he listened.
He gave Martin one more day to change his mind,
but as each stared fearlessly at the other at the end
of the second day's hearing they knew it was use-
less. As Martin walked out of the council chamber,
the cardinal picked up an unopened roll of parchment from the table and looked at it thoughtfully.

In the streets there was an excited hum of
conversation as Martin passed through the narrow,
twisting lanes. He knew he was being watched. The
cardinal's spies would not be likely to let him out
of their sight so that he could escape before the
next day. On the other hand, not all those who
looked at him were enemies. On the bookstalls he
could see printed copies of his own "Ninety-five
Theses", the statements he had put up at Witten-

berg. Rough men touched their heads or took off their hats respectfully as he passed. Martin smiled at them and spoke a friendly word—more friendly, so they said, than most of the monks you heard, who were only after money. A voice whispered as he passed, and he wondered if he had heard rightly.

"The cardinal won't get you to Rome, Doctor Luther—we'll see to that!" Martin looked round hastily, but no one seemed to have spoken. A group of Augsburg citizens were sitting outside the inn he had just passed, but none of them looked at him when he stared in their direction. He pulled his robes round him, and walked on, wondering.

* * *

The third day of the hearing came at last, after both Martin and Cajetan had had a sleepless night. Martin refused to recant—to admit he was wrong. The cardinal pointed out that unless he did so, he must go to Rome and stand his trial there. That, Martin knew well enough, though the cardinal did not mention it, meant death. He drew a deep breath, refused to give way, and was allowed to leave the chamber. The German princes and the bishops and priests watched him as he walked firmly from the room, his head steady and his eyes fearless. Then they turned to look at the cardinal. He was already opening the roll of parchment which had lain on his table throughout the trial.

Raising his hand, he motioned to one of his confidential servants and to a soldier who stood by him. The princes looked secretively at each other, nodding with pleased or anxious faces. Duke Frederick rose and left the room, sending a messenger to find Martin. The monk, however, was not to be found.

Almost as soon as the hearing in the council chamber was over the news spread through the town. It was late October, and darkness was falling quickly as a workman plucked Martin by the arm, and motioned him to follow down a narrow lane. Suddenly the man was joined by half a dozen others, all whispering at once.

"You know what will happen now, Doctor Luther . . ."

"The cardinal has orders to take you to Rome."

"He's had the Pope's letter about it on his table all through the trial . . ."

"Aye, he's sent out soldiers to arrest you, Doctor. Another hour in Augsburg and you'll be tied up in a cell. And that'll be the end of you."

"So we're getting you out while there's time."

Martin managed to cut into their excited words. "But what do you want me to do? And why should you bother to help me . . . this is just a quarrel in the Church."

A rough voice broke in. "Ah no, it isn't. It's a quarrel between Germany and the Pope . . . that's how we see it, anyway. It's time somebody stood up for us Germans."

"Time somebody stood up for common people like us against all the greedy monks and priests who are always after our money, too!"

Martin had no time to argue. In a way, these simple townsmen were right. It *was* part of what he was trying to do, to save ordinary people from ignorance and superstition, though he wanted to do much more than this. He longed for every man to know God for himself, and to find Him through the Bible rather than the Church. It was too late, now, to talk of things like this, for the men were pushing him down an even narrower alley-way which twisted down towards the walls of the town.

"There's friends outside with a horse, Doctor," said one of the group. "And a cloak and sword. Stirrups, too. You'll have to drop your robes when you're through the gate and turn yourself into a bright young nobleman!" A burst of laughter greeted the remark, and Martin joined in it.

The laughter came too soon, however, for they were hardly through the gate and Martin had scarcely put his hand on the horse's neck when one of the sentries shouted an angry challenge to them. He recognized the monk and remembered the order that had come to all the city guards. No monks must be allowed out of the city. Martin Luther must be held. There was a warrant for his arrest and a reward for anyone who caught him. The guard ran towards the men round the horse, brandishing his sword, but he was still twenty yards away from them when he saw the horse start forward, leaping as a man smacked its hind-quarters. Clinging to its back, without cloak, stirrups, spurs, breeches or sword, hunched up in his monk's robe and cowl, Martin heard the angry cries of the sentry and the laughter of the citizens growing fainter as he rode towards the distant safety of Wittenberg.

7

"HERE I STAND!"

IN the fading light of the December day the flames lit up the university courtyard, throwing huge shadows against the grey walls. The bonfire burned brightly, fresh sticks crackling as they were thrown on. The students stood solemnly round the square, tense with excitement.

"Martin Luther must be burned!" The words broke the silence, and there was a burst of laughter. If Martin were in Rome he might have been killed. They knew that well enough, for the Emperor, visiting Cologne, had invited him to come and talk with him and, when the monk did not arrive, he had burned all his books on a public bonfire. More than one Church leader had been heard to say that it would have been better if the troublesome monk himself had been thrown on to the fire instead of his books. Martin, however, was safe in Wittenberg, under the protection of Duke Frederick.

It was over two years since he had escaped from Augsburg, just when Cardinal Cajetan thought he would be able to fulfil his orders and carry him off, bound and under arrest, to Rome. Those who had helped him were neither punished nor caught.

Instead, a drawing was chalked on the walls of Augsburg and the homes of its leading citizens. It was a rough sketch of a *bundschuh*, the lace-up shoe which German peasants usually wore. The members of the council who had tried Luther knew very well what that meant. Over the years the peasants had grown to hate the Church leaders— and many of their masters were leading churchmen —because they felt themselves badly paid and ill-treated. Now, it was clear the members of the *Bundschuh* movement, the secret rebels, saw a leader in Martin Luther. Whatever the cardinal from Rome may have thought, the German bishops knew that if they were to attack Martin, the peasants would very probably rise on his side.

Back in his lodgings at Wittenberg, Martin sent a message to the Duke saying that he was willing to go away to France or Switzerland if Duke Frederick wished him to do so. The Council at Augsburg had said that the Duke must send his troublesome monk into exile, and Martin had no wish to make life more difficult for his generous patron. Duke Frederick replied that he would not send Martin away, nor even allow him to go. If the Emperor wanted him he would have to come and fetch him, and that would mean war. To his surprise, some of the leading German knights wrote to Martin offering him their help if he were attacked. Ulric von Hutten promised him his protection if he needed it and Franz von

Sickengen sent him a letter saying that a hundred knights would answer his call at any moment. Martin shook his head. He really wanted to get on with his work in the university and give time to preaching in the parish church, but it looked as if, against his own will, he were being turned into a new German leader. Knights and common people thought of him as their champion against the greedy demands of the Pope and his representatives, the cardinals and bishops, just as many monks and priests were already beginning to see him as a rebel against false ideas in religion. In his room at the university Martin began to explain what he thought, writing two or three very important books.

* * *

Soon they were being sold all over Germany. Martin was not only preaching against the evils of the Church, but he was writing against them as well. In Switzerland, Holland and France his books were bought as fast as they came into the tiny bookshops. A Swiss preacher, Zwingli, who believed as Martin did, bought six hundred of them and sent horsemen into the mountain villages to give them away to those who could read. From Rome itself a young monk who had been one of Martin's students in Wittenberg wrote to tell him that, in peril of their lives, his friends were distributing his writings throughout the city.

It was no wonder that the Pope once more issued an order. This time he demanded that Martin should come to Rome within sixty days and give himself up. If his opinions were found to be right, he would be set free. If they were wrong. . . . The "bull" did not go on to say what would happen to him, but it was not difficult to guess. The Pope's order was sent from Rome to Germany. Why it took so long to reach Martin nobody knows, but when it was at last brought to Wittenberg Martin opened it and read it without any sign of anxiety. He took it to his friends in the monastery.

"Do you see when it was written?" he asked.

"Why, it's dated three months ago!"

"Exactly. And I'm given two months to get to Rome. If I started *now* I should be a bit late!" Martin laughed as he put the parchment on the monastery table. "This isn't much use now, is it? Either to the Pope or to me?"

"What are you going to do with it?" asked one of his friends. "Send it back?"

"I thought," answered Martin, and they could see a smile in his eyes, "we might have a bonfire. There are a good many books here we don't need—and, after all, they did burn *my* books in Cologne." He looked round the room, walked across to the shelves and pulled down one or two books. "These, at any rate, don't teach the truth."

In the courtyard the bonfire was kindled, the

students crowded in and Martin dropped the books into the flames. Finally he stood for a moment or two watching the leaping fire, holding something in his hand. Then, with a gesture of contempt, he flung it into the middle of the flames. It was Martin's most complete act of rebellion against the Pope, for what he had burned was the Pope's letter summoning him to Rome. Almost at once the news of his action spread through the university and the city, and the students formed into a procession and marched round and round the town singing the *Te Deum* and other hymns.

*   *   *

Both the Pope and the Emperor were furiously angry. The Emperor, in particular, was frightened for he knew that war could very easily break out all over Germany between Luther's supporters and his own. He was worried as to whether he should leave Martin alone, or call him up for trial. If he did nothing, Martin's friends would grow stronger, and if he tried him and either had him killed or banished there could easily be a rebellion in which he would lose his own throne. It was not as if the common people alone thought of Martin as their friend; he had the support of many of the most powerful German knights, and Frederick of Saxony, who had brought Martin to his Wittenberg university and was one of the greatest princes in the country, stood firmly for the monk, even after he had burned the Pope's "bull".

At last, the Emperor Charles made up his mind. There was to be a "Diet"—that is, a council-meeting—of the German rulers in the town of Worms. The princes, the dukes, the bishops and the leading men from all over the German States would be gathered together. Charles determined to bring Martin to trial at the Diet itself. He sent an order to Wittenberg. The Duke looked at it carefully.

"Not even my brave monk is going to Worms without a safe-conduct," said Duke Frederick. "The Emperor must promise that he will come to no harm, and be allowed to return to Wittenberg, or I shall not allow him to leave my own territory!" The Emperor's letter went back, and was returned at last with a promise of safe-conduct. Even then, Martin's friends looked anxious.

"You shouldn't go, Martin. They're after your life, you know! Even if you get away from Worms after your trial, how do you know that you won't be kidnapped on the way back?"

"I don't know. Perhaps I shall be. Anyway, I have to go. I can't be a coward, writing books or preaching sermons here in the safety of Wittenberg and not stand up for what I know to be right in Worms. Why," he said grimly, " I would go even if there were as many devils waiting for me in Worms as there are tiles on the houses there!"

E

After that, there could be no arguing with him. In a cart that a local farmer lent him he set off with a few friends. Along the roads, men lifted their hats as he passed and women ran after the cart and asked him to bless them. "God keep you safe, Doctor Martin!" many of them shouted as he trundled on through the villages. Instead of a man going to his trial, it seemed like a man riding in triumph, and this was even more true when they reached the city gates of Worms. News of Martin's coming had gone ahead of him, and the Emperor's herald and a trumpeter were waiting at the gate to conduct him to his lodgings. They were not, however, the only people who waited for the brave monk. Outside the gateway, on top of the walls and pressing down the lanes that led into the main street was a huge mass of townsmen and villagers, two thousand of them, and as Martin's Saxon cart appeared on the muddy roadway a great cry went up from them all.

"Welcome to Worms! God keep you safe!" The crowd surged forward, almost knocking the Emperor's trumpeter and herald from their horses, and it was difficult for the cart to make its way through them to Martin's lodgings.

* * *

One thing was quite clear. It did not need the Emperor's promise to keep Martin safe in Worms. The loyalty of the ordinary people was enough for that. It would go hard with any man, prince or soldier, who tried to make him prisoner in Worms. Placards with the *bundschuh* stamped on them had already begun to appear overnight, and when it was time for Martin to be taken before the Diet the next day he was moved secretly through narrow by-lanes to avoid the crowd. For his own part, Martin was glad to be free of them, for this was not an argument between peasants and kings, with himself on the side of the workmen. It was something much deeper than that. He must stand by the truth as he had come to see it—that the Bible is God's word, that every man has the right to read it for himself, that God has no need of penance or purgatory before He will forgive people, that in many things the Pope and his counsellors were wrong, and simple godly people were right.

The year was 1521, ten years after Martin had first gone to Wittenberg. He had begun a movement which would grow stronger and stronger. He had made his "protest" against the wrongs of the Roman Catholic Church, and already men thought of him as the first great "protestant". In the days that followed Europe was to be divided between those who followed Luther and his fellow-reformers, who would be called "Protestants", and those who stood by the Pope, the Catholics who were loyal to Rome. Much as he hated the idea of splitting the Church, Martin knew he could not give in to those who argued with him at Worms. Facing the Emperor, the princes, the leaders of the Church, his voice rang out across the council chamber.

"Here I stand. I can do no other. So help me God!"

From that moment, he was a marked man. Safe though he was in Worms where so many of the citizens stood by him, it was a long ride to the security of Wittenberg. Setting off for home once more in the Saxon cart, Martin knew nothing of the armed men who waited patiently for him to come to the lonelier part of the forest.

8

PRISONER IN THE WARTBURG

VERY slowly the cart rolled along the road towards the forest. At Worms, the townsfolk had lined the streets, waving good-bye and good luck to their hero. Now and again, as he passed through the country villages, the peasants who had wished Martin God-speed and safety doffed their hats to him and bowed, and the monk blessed them as he went by. With his few companions he discussed the future. Almost certainly many monks and nuns would now leave the monasteries. They would probably want to have their services in German instead of Latin. They might easily try and get rid of the images and relics from their churches. It would undoubtedly be a time of difficulty.

"You're going to have your work cut out, trying to hold the rebels against Rome from doing anything silly," remarked one of Martin's fellow-monks.

"The trouble is," replied Martin, "that I shan't have time to do what I really want to do—the most important thing of all."

"What's that?"

"Turn the Bible into German. How many of our

common people—the men and women in the
streets of Worms or in those villages we've gone
through—could read it in Latin? Not one in a
thousand! And yet that's the only Bible they've
got."

His companions turned to him in excitement.
"It's a wonderful idea, Martin."

"But that will turn the Church leaders against
you more than ever. They say ordinary people
should not be *allowed* to read the Bible."

"And *I* say," answered Martin, thumping the
side of the cart, "they will never be real
Christians until they are able to read it all for
themselves."

"But will you be able to do it? It's a terrific job,
Martin, and you never seem to have time for all the
things you want to do now!"

Before Martin could answer, there was a shout
from the driver of the cart, and the monks sprang
up in alarm, almost falling out as they swayed
unsteadily about. In their interest in what Martin
was saying they had hardly noticed that they had
entered the forest. Now, from the shadow of the
trees, a group of armed knights had sprung
forward, grasped the bridle of the horse, and
dragged the driver to the ground. The monks, like
the driver, were quite unarmed and it was hopeless
to resist. The only man the ambush appeared to be
interested in was Martin himself. Tying his
hands behind him, they heaved him on to a rider-

less horse and galloped off through the trees, down a series of narrow, twisting paths.

They refused to answer any of Martin's questions, and even when the twilight turned to darkness they went on riding without even stopping for food. Back in the forest, the monks got sadly into the cart once more and drove slowly on to Wittenberg with the news that Martin had been kidnapped by an armed gang hired by his enemies.

Martin himself was sore and angry when, almost at midnight, after a long, dangerous climb up into the hills, he saw the outlines of a fortified castle against the starry sky. The gate opened at a cry from the commander of the armed band, the whole group of horsemen trotted through into the courtyard beyond, and the gate clanged behind them. Somebody untied the ropes that bound Martin's hands and helped him from his horse. He looked for a moment at the high walls, the groups of soldiers and the closed gate, wondering if it would be worth trying to escape. In despair, he shrugged his shoulders and followed his captors. He had seen the last of the world outside the castle, though he did not know it, for many months to come.

*   *   *

As he entered the building itself, he wondered what was going to happen to him. It was in places like this that the enemies of the Emperor disappeared. Nothing would be easier, considering the cliffs which fell steeply from the walls, or the dungeons which lay below his feet. For a moment, he was blinded by the light of torches stuck against the stone walls. Then, as he saw more clearly, he started in amazement as a man stepped towards him. He had seen him often in Wittenberg, and knew him for one of the trusted councillors of Duke Frederick the Wise himself. For some reason that he could not understand, Duke Frederick had changed sides, and had him kidnapped.

The Duke's representative bowed in front of him, and Martin listened in bewilderment as he spoke.

"I am sorry we had to save you this way, Dr. Luther."

"*Save* me?"

"Naturally. You didn't think Duke Frederick had any evil intentions towards you, surely? Oh no, no! You've been kidnapped for your own safety, Doctor. Only, you see, it had to be done properly. It would be no use allowing people to recognize your captors as the Duke's men. So far as most people are concerned—you've just disappeared. No one will have the least idea who has spirited you away."

"But why?"

"Because you've been condemned as a heretic. Your life isn't worth that much"—he snapped his fingers—"at the moment."

"Where am I?"

"You're in one of the Duke's castles, Doctor Martin. The Wartburg—one of the most inaccessible of them all. You're to stay here for the time being . . . a few months perhaps, even a year. By that time the world may be safer for you." He smiled in a friendly way. "You've been looking very tired lately; trying to do too many jobs. This will be a chance for you to rest. There must be some work—some writing—you specially want to do, surely? This is the time to get on with it." He turned away, motioning Martin to follow him. "For the moment, after a ride like that, all you need is plenty to eat and a long sleep."

*　　*　　*

In the months that followed a great many people wondered what had happened to the rebellious monk. Some people were sure the Emperor had had him killed; others thought he had been spirited away to Rome. Then it became clear that, wherever he was, he was safe and well, for leaflets and books with his name on them began to appear. They were bought almost before they were on the bookstalls. In his absence Martin became an even greater figure than he had been during the previous years. It was becoming clear now what the result of some of his "protests" would be, and as members of the Duke's forces came from time to time to the Wartburg they brought news of what was happening in Wittenberg and some of the other German cities.

"Philip Melanchthon has completely changed the way of giving Holy Communion—he doesn't say the Mass any longer."

"A dozen or more monks have left the Augustinian monastery."

"It's said that some of the monks are even talking about getting married, in spite of their vows to remain single all their lives."

The news made Martin restive in his big room with the thick stone walls and the long view over the forests, but he could do nothing about it. He was under orders not to go back to Wittenberg at any cost, though it was unlikely that anyone would know him if he did. Not even the soldiers of the guard knew who he was. To them, he was a knight who had hidden from his enemies. The monk's habit had been rolled up and put away, and his shaven head was now covered with dark curly hair. He had a thick beard, and wore a red woollen coat and a sword-belt. It was not fear of the consequences, however, which kept him where he was, but the task at which he was working. On the table in his room were spread out piles of paper, heaps of books, many of them in Latin and the most important ones of all in Greek. The soldiers who came to talk to him shrugged their shoulders as they looked at the strange knight turning these books into German which they could understand.

He was a clever chap, this man who had run away from the world, but why he should spend his time on such tasks they simply could not understand. It would have amazed them if they had been told that what was being written there would change the life of Germany.

Martin slept badly, tumbling out of bed in the earliest hours of daylight to get on with his work. Then, at last, it was finished. He looked at the pile of paper, and gave a deep sigh of relief. Then taking another piece of paper he wrote, in German, *The New Testament*. The first part of his task was ended. Though the leaders of the Church, the Pope and the bishops, would be furious that such a thing had been done, he had translated the New Testament out of Greek and Latin into the language of the people. When it was printed, as it soon would be, monks and cobblers, princesses and peasants' wives, and the little children of every city and village in the country, would be able to read God's word for themselves.

"One day," said Martin to himself, "I shall have to do the Old Testament, too. That won't be so easy, but I'll do it before I die!"

*   *   *

By secret ways the manuscript was taken to the printers and Martin was uneasy until he knew that it was actually in their hands. Now, with the most important thing done, and a great many lesser books and pamphlets written, Martin fumed and fretted in the out-of-the-way castle, wondering what to do. More than anything he wanted to get back to Wittenberg, but Duke Frederick had sent him a special message telling him to stay where he was. Then, at last, news came which forced him to make up his mind.

A few days later there rode in through the town gate of Wittenberg a black-bearded knight, with a sword clanging against his stirrups. No one took much notice of him as he steered his horse through the people and urged it towards the castle church. When he jumped from it and flung the reins to a small boy the lad bowed swiftly, calling him "my lord". One or two monks glanced at him as he strode into the building and looked round, but there was no sign of recognition in their faces or amongst the students who watched him curiously. Anger flamed in his eyes as he turned round. On the ground lay bits of plaster, some of them coloured with gold, red and blue. Against a pillar, as if it had been thrown there, was the smashed head and shoulders of a saint's statue which had stood near the pulpit.

It was true, then, the things he had heard! He was glad to know that the people wanted reforms in the Church, but sorry that they should turn to violence. Even while he was standing there in the church, the noise of a rioting crowd grew louder and, striding to the door, he saw a group of monks hurrying with what dignity they could keep in front of an angry crowd who pelted them with stones and refuse. As some of the rioters ran into the church, hoping to find other monks to be tormented, the black-bearded knight moved back to the chancel steps, mounted them and looked down on the noisy crowd.

"Stop this at once!" he ordered.

It was the voice rather than the words which silenced the people. There was a familiar note about it, despite the disguising garments.

"Who are you, that you dare to speak to us like that?" came a voice from the crowd. "Don't you know about the reforms in the Church? Don't you know that this is Luther's city?"

The knight drew himself up as he answered. "*I* am Martin Luther, my friends—and I think it is time, after all, that I came back to Wittenberg and taught you how to behave!"

9

WITTENBERG ONCE MORE

"STAY where you are!"

Martin listened to the message from Duke Frederick, and muttered angrily in reply. He was back in the Wartburg once more, but the promise he had made during his brief visit to Wittenberg was constantly in his mind. He had only spent two days in his old city, but that was enough to show him that events had got out of hand. He knew he was needed there and had promised to come back by Easter. Now the Duke had sent him a sharp command to remain in hiding in the lonely inaccessible castle where he had already spent the greater part of a year.

"His Excellency says you are to remain in the Wartburg, Doctor Luther. If you return to Wittenberg, if you will excuse my saying so, you will make trouble for everybody!"

Martin smiled for a moment. He knew what lay behind the message. The Duke had protected him, but he was still trying to keep in favour with the Emperor. He was not convinced that Martin's new ideas were all true, though he could see the sense of many of them. Mass was still said in the Wittenberg churches and services were held in

Latin instead of German. Indulgences were still asked for and paid for by the hundreds of pilgrims who came to see the Duke's relics. Those who broke the law by smashing images or rioting in the churches were severely punished. Duke Frederick was unwilling to support a rebel against the authority of Rome. It was easier to keep him out of sight in an isolated castle. With Martin out of the way, the Duke did not have to take sides in the argument which was beginning to split the Church in Germany and other parts of Europe.

"And then, of course, my good Doctor, there is Duke George!" The messenger looked serious and spread out his hands in a helpless gesture. "If *you* come back and our own Duke is forced to take your side, what do you think *he* will do?"

Martin knew very well what Duke George of Saxony would like to do. His lands adjoined Duke Frederick's own. His state university at Leipzig had lost many students to Wittenberg since Luther had become a professor there. He was a determined enemy of all that Martin stood for and a firm supporter of the Pope and the Roman Catholic Emperor. Martin turned to the messenger. "What do *you* think he would do?" he asked.

The messenger shrugged his shoulders. "He would *like* to have the Emperor's orders to march into Wittenberg. If you were there it would be a good excuse. Duke Frederick, of course, will never give you up willingly, and if our enemy was ordered to capture you it would mean war."

Martin paced up and down the room. He could easily enough see how his protector felt about all this, and yet he knew that he must do what was right. "I'll write to His Excellency," he told the messenger, "and let him know how I feel." The man bowed, and they began to talk of other things. Martin told him that his translation of the New Testament was already being printed, and that he was busy working on other books and pamphlets which he wanted to finish before Easter. The Duke's messenger told him how, all over Germany, men were coming to regard him as the leader of a new kind of Church. In Wittenberg, Carlstadt and Philip Melanchthon were the leaders of the reforming movement. In Switzerland, Ulrich Zwingli was also speaking out about the truth of the Bible and the errors of the Church of Rome. Martin could not avoid seeing that when he had hammered his poster on the door of Wittenberg church he had begun a movement which was going to begin a new kind of Church. For a long time, he had hoped that the Pope and the bishops would see that he was right and would change the evils of the Church for themselves. Now, it was clear, that would not happen. Much against his own will, for he loved a great many things in the Church where he had grown up, he was leading people away from the Roman Catholic Church into an entirely new Church.

When the messenger had gone, Martin sat down to write to his protector. He knew now what he must say. If the new movement was not to get out of hand he himself was needed, not at the Wartburg, but where things were happening. If Duke George made his presence an excuse for starting war against Duke Frederick that would be very sad, but. . . . He picked up his quill pen, dipped it in the big ink-well and began to write.

"I once said, your Excellency," he wrote swiftly, "that if there were as many devils in Worms as there were tiles on its house-roofs, I would still go there. I now say that even if it rains Duke Georges for nine days on end over Wittenberg, I will come back by Easter!"

*   *   *

The traveller who rode towards the university city a month or two later was once more dressed like a knight, with beard, sword and spurs, but under his arm he carried a heavy book. When he could let the horse take its own time, he read as he rode, keeping a light hand on the reins. A stranger who stayed the night with him at an inn was astonished when he found the book was written not only in a foreign language but even in letters which he had never seen before. He was even more amazed when he found that the knight was reading, as he imagined, from the back of the book towards the front, instead of the normal way.

"What is it that you're reading, sir?" he asked.

"Eh?" The "knight" looked up at his companion and blinked. "Oh—I'm sorry. I was trying to think how I could turn that verse into our modern German. It's the Old Testament."

"The Old Testament? But . . . er . . . that's written in Latin, surely. And we're not allowed to read it. The bishops say so. Only the priests and monks can do that." He sniffed. "Judging by the way some of them live it would do them good if they read it a bit more often!"

"This is the Old Testament as it was originally written—in Hebrew, sir, not Latin."

"And you can read it?"

"Aye, and turn it into German, too, sir. Listen to this." The "knight" pointed to a passage and, running his fingers along the lines of strange letters, began to translate it as he went. His companion listened enthralled.

"My dear sir, you're an odd knight and no mistake. You ought to turn it *all* into German. Now that that fellow Luther has led a rebellion against the Pope and told people to read the Bible for themselves, there's plenty of people who'd buy it, you know." He looked sharply at the man with the book. "I suppose you're not a friend of his, are you?" He flicked his fingers to the landlord of the inn to order some more food. "Funny thing, where Luther disappeared to, isn't it?"

"He'll be back!"

"You think so?"

"I know he will be. He'll be in Wittenberg in a day or so." He picked up his Hebrew book, bowed farewell and crossed to the narrow stairs, smiling as he went. The stranger had spoken more truly than he knew, for the "knight", of course, was Martin Luther himself, on his way back home, still disguised against attack from his enemies on the road—and one of the reasons he had determined to settle down at Wittenberg rather than some other city was that he might claim the help of his scholar-friends in translating the Old Testament into German, so that his people might have the whole Bible in their own tongue.

* * *

At first, back in Wittenberg, he was given a warm welcome by most of the townspeople and students, and a cold one by the Duke. In time, both attitudes changed towards him. The peasants hoped that Martin would be their champion when they rebelled against their landlords, for it seemed as if he would naturally support the common people. Instead, he stood aside from the "Peasants' Rebellion" which broke out soon after his return, and many of those who had been his supporters turned their backs on him. They did not return to the Roman Church, however, but joined other Reformers who went much further in their thinking than Martin Luther himself.

Martin was no longer a lonely man, fighting against a corrupt Church. All over Europe, in England and Scotland as well as on the Continent, there were those who thought as he did. When they could not get the reforms they wanted inside the Church, they broke away from it so that, all over the place, new branches of the Church, or denominations, began to spring up. There were Lutherans in Germany, Calvinists in Switzerland, a new Church of England, and what was to become Presbyterianism in Scotland. They were the "Protestant Churches" which, in time, would be as strong and as big as the Roman Catholic Church from which they had broken away. At the same time, Martin's protest against the evils of his old Church was having an effect there, too, for already there were many people who knew that he was right and, though they did not wish to leave the Roman Church as he had been forced to do, set themselves to get rid of many of the evil things against which Martin and his friends had objected.

When Duke Frederick saw that, far from being alone, he would have the support of other princes, he came down firmly on Martin's side. Wittenberg became the centre of the Lutheran Reformation. By 1525, eight years after Martin had nailed his famous "theses" to the church door, the Mass was ended in the Wittenberg churches, and services were being held in German instead of Latin. The Duke had turned out his huge collection of holy relics, for which he had paid so much money and travelled so many thousands of miles. There were no more "indulgences" to be had in the city, and men were taught to ask for and take God's forgiveness themselves instead of through the priests.

By that time, too, Martin's translation of the New Testament had been published for three years, and was being bought as quickly as it could be printed. In the meanwhile, Martin had turned to writing hymns, putting into verse the beliefs he tried to preach. His hymnbook was even more widely bought than his German New Testament, and housewives, farmers and merchants sang his hymns to their simple tunes all over the land.

The life of the Church was changing, too. Monks and nuns were leaving their cloisters and going to find work in the busy world outside. While he was still in the Wartburg, Martin had heard to his amazement that the priest of the castle church in Wittenberg had broken his vows and got married. Now, more and more monks were coming from the quiet cloisters, putting on ordinary clothes, marrying and settling down into the sort of houses in which half the people of Germany lived.

Martin looked on and smiled tolerantly. He was busy all day and all night—too busy, very often, to undress when he went to bed, so that he simply flung himself down and went to sleep. There were innumerable letters to be written, people to be seen, questions to be answered. He wrote more and more books and pamphlets, lectured on the Bible and preached on Sundays and week-days. There was no time for a wife or a family in a life like Martin's. He had had his fortieth birthday, and laughed loudly when one of his friends suggested that, monk though he had been, he needed a wife to look after him and keep him in order.

"I'm too old, too busy and too happy," replied Martin. "You won't catch *me* getting married!"

10

SAFE STRONGHOLD

THE covered wagon rolled along the road from
Wittenberg as it had done month by month
for many years. Even a blind beggar—and there
were plenty on the German roads—would have
known whose it was, for the smell of fish clung to
it, even when there were no barrels rattling about
inside. The only unusual thing on this particular
occasion was that Leonard Kopp, the prosperous
owner, was driving it himself instead of letting one
of his workmen do it. Perhaps, said those who
looked twice at him, the convent was slow in
paying up and Herr Kopp was going to try and
collect his money.

Kopp had for years delivered barrels of herrings
to a convent some miles away. The nuns had to
buy their fish for Lent and their Friday meals,
since they could not catch them themselves,
and Kopp had done well from the trade. The only
question in the mind of the convent authorities at
that moment was whether they ought to go on
dealing with a Lutheran sympathizer, or not.
Since his herrings had always been good, it was not
difficult to decide. This time, as he drove along,
Kopp wondered if they would go on trading with

him after the day's dealings were over. He intended
to bring away more than he took in.

The wagon drew up in the convent yard, and the
driver backed the horse almost up to the doorway
through which the herring-barrels were carried in.
The nuns themselves, strong-armed from the
heavy work they had to do, heaved the barrels into
the kitchen, and then flung back into the cart a
clattering load of empty barrels from the visit
before. The driver backed even nearer to the door.
Anyone watching would have said they were taking
longer than usual to load the empty casks, and
when at last Kopp cracked his whip and the horse
drew away it seemed to find the load at least as
heavy to pull as the full fish-barrels had been. In a
minute or two they were out of the courtyard and
on the road to Wittenberg. From the wagon,
amongst the barrels, came a strangely human
noise and the driver spoke loudly and angrily.

"If you don't want to have us all arrested and
see me killed—*keep quiet* in there!" With an
anxious look on his face, he flicked the horse
sharply with his whip in a vain effort to make it
walk a little faster.

* * *

Burgher Kopp was not the only worried man
that morning. In Wittenberg Martin paced to and
fro, waiting anxiously for the fish-merchant's
arrival. Between them they had done something

dangerous and criminal, and when at last the covered cart rattled over the cobbles of the old city Martin heaved a sigh of relief. It stopped at last, in a secluded quarter of the town, and Martin, who had followed it from the city gate, helped to lift down the empty barrels and then rather more gently helped out the twelve young nuns who had escaped from the convent amongst the fish-casks. A few straggling passers-by watched with wide-open eyes as the girls almost fell out of the wagon, one after another.

"Doctor Martin has done it this time!" muttered one of the onlookers. "He's been abducting nuns—and he should know that to steal a nun from a convent, or even to help her to escape, means the death penalty."

The man's friend nodded. "H'm. That's right. If it were in Duke George's land he'd be killed for it, sure enough. I don't know about our Duke Frederick, though."

"Ah well, friend, we all know they're still hoping to catch him and burn him anyway, so perhaps he isn't very worried about a little thing like stealing a dozen nuns!"

The men were right, except that the nuns had written to Martin and asked him to arrange for them to escape from the convent. They had come to believe in the Protestant way, but did not dare tell the Mother Superior of the convent what they thought. Martin relied on his own protector not taking so strict a view of the business as the Catholic princes would do, though he knew that not even Frederick the Wise liked men who broke the law. However, it was true that he was expecting to be taken prisoner any day and burned at the stake, and one more "crime" would not make much difference. Already the first Protestant martyrs in Belgium had been burned for their faith. It was partly because of these things that Martin had made up his mind that he would never follow the example of some of his other friends and get married. Besides that, he had never seen anyone he really wanted to marry.

When he looked at the nuns that day, after their uncomfortable ride in the cart, he saw no one to make him change his mind, though he knew that the safest thing for most of them would be to marry and set up home. Then, no one would be able to take them back to the nunnery.

*　　*　　*

In the end, three of the nuns went to their own homes, eight others got married and one, Katherine von Bora, was left. It had been arranged that she should marry a young nobleman who was studying at the university, but his family objected. Then Martin picked another husband for her and she objected so strongly to him that she refused to marry him whatever happened.

"Dr. Luther! Really, I wouldn't dream of it!

Why, I would rather marry you yourself than him!"

It was a little later that Martin went home to see his mother and father, now both of them old people. He was telling them about his adventure with the nuns, and laughing over Katherine's remark. His father leaned forward and tapped him on the knee. "Well, my lad—why don't you do what she says? Eh?"

Martin looked startled and a little frightened. "Whatever do you mean, sir?"

"Why—marry the girl, of course. I know you think you're too old, but it'd do you a lot of good. It's time you had someone to look after you, my boy!"

"Well, I really hadn't thought of it." Martin laughed, and the noise almost rocked his parents' small kitchen. "I've been so busy getting other people married that I've not given much time to setting up a home of my own."

"You need a home, Martin, my boy. This business of priests and monks living without homes and children is all wrong. You need somewhere that you can relax—somewhere you can feel safe, a safe stronghold against all your enemies in the world outside. And, Heaven knows, you've got plenty of them!"

Probably because of this talk with his father, Martin made up his mind. He sent a letter to Burgher Leonard Kopp, who had helped the nuns to escape. "A miracle has happened," it read, "and I'm going to get married. Mind you come to the wedding!" Not only Kopp, but all Wittenberg turned out to see the great event. A band of pipers marched through the streets at the head of a long procession of friends and guests, leading Martin and Katherine to the church where, in the porch with everyone watching them, the marriage ceremony took place, and then led them still further to the Augustinian monastery, where there was a banquet set for all who would come.

*   *   *

Martin's fears about his arrest, followed by being burned to death, came to nothing, largely because he never again moved away from the part of Germany where he had settled, and where he had so many supporters. In his crowded, noisy home at Wittenberg he went on with his work for twenty years after he was married, dying there when he was something over sixty years old. These twenty years were very different from the dangerous times through which Martin had passed since his visit to Rome. He was now famous, one of the best-known men in Germany. His books were read all over Europe, and his hymns sung wherever German was spoken. As a result, wise men and students crowded to Wittenberg to see him.

It was not easy for Katherine. When they

were married they had no money at all between them, apart from what their friends gave them, and however hard·Martin worked, they never seemed to have very much throughout the years that followed. Martin got no profits from the books he wrote, and more than once he tried working at some craft or other, such as carpentry, in order to make ends meet. But he soon got tired, and was always too busy at other more important things, and the money he spent on lathes or tools was wasted. It was fortunate that he had so many generous friends, or they would hardly have been able to live at all. The Duke gave over to them the cloister where Martin had lived in the monastery, and often sent them gifts of game, wine or money. The real trouble was that, unless Katherine got it first, Martin gave away all the money to the beggars and the students who always seemed to be crowded round the door of their house.

As soon as Katherine got the household out of debt, Martin was short of money once more. He said he never worried about bills, because as soon as he paid one, another arrived. The real trouble was that, having lived much of his life in the monastery, he had never had to worry about money and had not a practical mind at all. Instead, he was always talking, reading, preaching, and planning the next book he was going to write or the next series of lectures he would have to deliver.

Where he and Katherine managed to put everyone in the house was something of a mystery. Very soon there were six children belonging to Martin and Katherine, but even so the house was always crowded with students, for Martin lectured regularly and used his home as a students' hostel for the university. Some of these young men wrote down many of Martin's sayings, for he could hardly stop talking and much that he said was both wise and witty. The sayings were published later in a book called *Luther's Table Talk*.

*　　*　　*

Looking back over the centuries, we can see what a heroic figure this rebellious monk really was. He had the courage to defy the whole Church and face death itself for what he believed to be true. He freed men from ignorance and superstition. He "protested"—that is, "proclaimed"—God's truth as it is given to us in the Bible and, so that men might see for themselves, translated the whole Bible into his people's own tongue. He forced the Roman Catholic Church to drive out many of the evils that had crept into it. He stood firmly for religious liberty—the right of men to speak and worship as they knew they ought. In all this struggle, he was often ill. He slept badly, suffered from dreadful depression and sickness, and in spite of the love of his family and friends, felt terribly lonely. There were long periods when he wondered whatever was going to happen to them all, and could not believe that he could live in safety to the end of his life. Though he was worried for himself, he was even more worried about his family. Yet one thing was certain. He had done what God wanted him to do, and God would never desert him.

A year or two after his marriage he wrote a hymn which swept across Germany, and which is still sung all over the world. To the end of his life, Martin would sing it or repeat it to himself, and the older he grew the more true it seemed to be.

> "A safe stronghold our God is still,
>   A trusty shield and weapon;
> He'll help us clear from all the ill
>   That hath us now o'ertaken . . .
>
> And were this world all devils o'er,
>   And watching to devour us,
> We lay it not to heart so sore;
>   Not they can overpower us . . .
>
> And though they take our life,
>   Goods, honour, children, wife,
> Yet is their profit small:
>   These things shall vanish all;
> The city of God remaineth!"